THE GREAT WONDERS OF THE AMAZON

Northwater

CONSTANTINE ISSIGHOS

Copyright 2012 © Constantine Issighos. Published in Canada. Printed in U.S.A. No part of this book may be reproduced or transmitted in any form or by any means, electronic or mechanical, including photocopying, recording, and/or by any information storage and retrieval system except by a reviewer who may quote brief passages in a review to be printed in a magazine, newspaper, or on the web without written permission in writing from the author/publisher. For information, please contact www.awaqkunabooks.com

NorthWater is an imprint of Awaqkuna Books Inc.

Vol. 13 of THE AMAZON EXPLORATION SERIES:
THE GREAT WONDERS OF THE AMAZON

Library and Archives Canada

ISBN 978-0-9878601-2-5

Library and Archives Canada Cataloguing in Publication

ATTENTION CHILDRENS ASSOCIATIONS, BOOK STORES, PUBLIC OR PRIVATE LIBRARIES: quantity discounts are available on bulk purchases of this book series.

THE AMAZON EXPLORATION SERIES

Children's Books
by
Constantine Issighos

1. Upper Amazon Voyage by River Boat
2. The People of the River
3. The Children of the River
4. Amazon's Nature of Things
5. Echoes of Nature: a Beautiful Wild Habitat
6. The Amazon Rainforest
7. Amazonian Sisterhood
8. Amazon River Wolves
9. Amazonian Landscapes and Sunsets
10. Amazonian Canopy: the Roof of the World's Rainforest
11. Amazonian Tribes: a World of Difference
12. Birds, Flowers and Butterflies of the Amazon
13. The Great Wonders of the Amazon
14. The Jaguar People
15. The Fresh Water Giants
16. The Call of the Shaman
17. Indigenous Families: Life in Harmony with Nature
18. Amazon in Peril
19. Giant Tarantulas and Centipedes
20. The Amazon Ethno-Botanical Garden
21. The Real Amazon Tribal Warriors

The immense biodiversity of the Amazon rainforest may have been the consequence of catastrophic events. Rather than being a stable geological system, the Amazon rainforest—including the river and its tributaries—is in a constant process of rejuvenation and change. However, such geological changes are far from being disastrous to animal and vegetative life in the Amazon basin. Current and past moderate climatic disturbances have actually helped account for the splendid biological diversity of the Amazon.

Current evidence also sheds a light on the great wonders and mystery of the prehistoric Amazon. In this unknown prehistoric past lies the origin of the diversity of the richest ecosystem on our planet today. The current prevailing view is that species gathered in the warm and humid environment to avoid the danger of freezing during the Ice Age, about 15 million years ago. A cradle of natural evolution, the region has allowed species to evolve slowly, producing the fantastic biodiversity present today.

The Amazon rainforest is characterized by a unique tree structure of several horizontal layers including the overstory, then the canopy, the understory, the shrub layer and the forest floor. The overstory is 30-40meters (120 to 150 feet) above the forest floor. The canopy refers to the dense roof of leaves and tree branches formed by closely spaced trees. In the canopy there are multiple branch levels and leaves known collectively as the understory. Ground vegetation in the rainforest is minimal and consists mainly of vines and tree seedlings.

The Amazon River measures 6,400 kilometres (4,000 miles) from its source to its mouth. It is ranked as the largest in watershed area, number of tributaries and volume of water discharge. Thus the Amazon River is the most voluminous river on Earth, eleven times the volume of the Mississippi river. The southern Peruvian Andean mountains are the source of the Ucayali and Apurimac Rivers which join together just south of Nauta to form the Amazon. The Amazon River drains an area equivalent to the United States—34 million to 120 million litres of fresh water per second. Roughly half of the discharge is in Brazil; the rest is shared by Peru, Ecuador, Bolivia and Venezuela. The annual outflow from the river accounts for a fifth of all the freshwater that drains into the world's oceans. In fact, the outpouring of freshwater is so vast that the salt content of the Atlantic Ocean is altered for a distance of about 330 kilometres (220 miles) from the mouth of the river.

The following brief list by no means even touches the fringes of the immense biodiversity in animal and plant life that exists in the Amazon basin.

Red Howler Monkey

The Red Howler Monkey lives in the canopy of the Amazon rainforest. Typical of monkeys, red howlers are very social and live in groups ranging from 5 to 35 members led by a dominant male. Although when you look up you may not be able to see them in the canopy, you sure can hear them, for they make the loudest howling sound in the forest. Their diet includes fruits, flowers, leaves, small birds, reptiles and mammals.

Jaguar

The Jaguar is a carnivorous predator whose diet includes capybaras, snakes, deer, monkeys, peccaries, rodents, armadillos, birds and other small mammals. The jaguar is an excellent nocturnal hunter with superb hearing; it can pick up a prey's movement even before it sees the animal.

Of all the Amazonian land predators, the jaguar is the most water loving. It can crack tortoise and turtle shells with its powerful jaws, and can use its claws to fish and climb trees. A jaguar yellowish fur has large circles with small spots inside them called *rosettes*.

Arapaima

Arapaima has the largest scales of any freshwater fish in the world. These extremely large scales are edged in bright red pigment forming an array of fine, diagonal stripe-like markings. It is truly one of a kind and not likely to be mistaken for anything else in the Amazon. It can be found in the Amazon river and its tributaries in Brazil, Peru, Colombia and Ecuador.

Arapaima can reach over 270 kilos (600 lbs) and over 6 meters (14 feet) long. At this length, Arapaima is rare because they have become a favourite of the urban fish gourmet. Arapaima must periodically surface to gulp air. Oxygen is absorbed by a vascularised air bladder where CO_2 is exchanged via air gills. The Arapaima is very adaptable and has successfully been transplanted outside of the Amazon.

Giant Otters

Giant otters—*Lobo de Rio* (River Wolf)—are the largest of the freshwater otters living in the rivers, canals and lakes of Brazil, Bolivia, Ecuador and Peru They are the rarest and most endangered of the otter species and it is estimated that there are less than 5,000 on South America continent.

Besides their large size of 1.8 meters (almost 6 feet), Giant Otters are characterized by the irregular patches of light fur on their chests and their noisy, gregarious behaviour. Historical records from South America show there were once massive Giant Otters reaching 2.5 meters (8 feet) in length before the species was hunted to near extinction.

Red Bellied Piranha

The piranhas are a group of carnivorous freshwater fish living in the Amazon River and its tributaries. They are known for their sharp teeth and their aggressive appetite for meat and flesh. Some species of piranhas have extremely broad geographical ranges, living in the rivers of Guyana, Paraguay and Panama and in the Sao Francisco river system of Brazil. Other species appear to have a much more limited distribution.

They are normally about 15 to 25 cm long (6 to 10 inches) although some up to 40 cm (24 inches) in length have been found. Regardless of their notorious reputation, ecologically piranhas are important components of the rainforest environment. As both predators and scavengers, piranhas influence the local distribution and composition of fish assemblages. Certain piranha species consume large quantities of seeds and function as dispersers. Among the piranha's natural predators are Pink Dolphin, Black Caimans and humans.

Freshwater Pink Dolphins

The Amazonian Pink Dolphin lives in the river systems of Brazil, Peru and Venezuela. Visitors who travel the river by boat can enjoy seeing the dolphins performing their skilful manoeuvres as they follow the vessel.

Since its neck vertebrae are not fused together, the Pink Dolphin is able to bend its neck in a 90 degree angle to its body. Their favoured prey is the notorious piranha that exists in the same waters.

Inhabitants of the Amazon Rainforest

The Amazon has a long history of human settlement. Large and sedentary communities of great social complexity have existed in the Amazon rainforest for millennia. Inhabitants cleared sections of the rainforest for farming and managed the forest to maintain a balanced distribution of animal life for domestic consumption.

There are people with two different heritages living in the rainforest—the mestizos and the indigenous. Inhabitants with Spanish ancestors—mestizos—tend to live along the riverbanks of the rainforest. They live in small villages or small farm plots; they speak Spanish with a Spanish accent and have dark skin and hair. They wear clothes similar to North Americans or Europeans in warm climates. They live a simple life, usually cooking outside with charcoal; they eat whatever they can find in the forest or the river, what they grow on their small plots or what they trade for in the city.

The indigenous people are natives to the land—their ancestors have lived in the Amazon rainforest for thousands of years. They have their own language or dialect, cultural traditions and mystical ceremonies. Indigenous craftsmen make wood carvings, necklaces, simple dolls, flutes, woven baskets, blowguns and bows and arrows.

In general, the indigenous people do not have a monetary system. Rather, they barter for items such as clothing and fabrics, red lipstick or metal items. They also trade in fish, wild meat and products from the land. Some of these items they keep for themselves and some they barter for supplies with other indigenous or mestizos who travel up or down the Amazon River.

The river is very important to the lives of the 'river people." There are no roads in the forest and the rivers are their main form of transportation. Adults and "children of the river" travel by dugout canoes that are carved by hand from hardwood trees. Children as young as 6 years old know how to paddle a canoe.

The children of the river attend school in villages along the riverbanks. A typical school is a one-room building where a teacher teaches students in many grades. Usually the teacher lives in a house near the school, which is painted deep blue so people can identify it easily. Most schools are poor, which means that they do not have enough supplies for students.

Medicinal Plants

For thousands of years, indigenous people have lived in harmony with the rainforest, living off of the plants and animals in their environment. Their relationship with the Amazon is very intimate; they are connected in every way. The plants are their curative friends, for whom they have great respect. The flora and fauna provide everything they need, including medicine.

Medicinal plants pre-date mankind. Undoubtedly, animals used them to heal themselves also. We as human beings are made of the same basic DNA material as the life around us. Humans breathe out carbon dioxide and plants breathe it in. Plants breathe out oxygen and humans breathe it in. Where would we be without plants?

The indigenous cultures of the Amazon have used plants for ritual healing ceremonies and religious observances for millennia. The plants' curative properties are regarded as good or bad spiritual entities. The Shaman use medicinal plants to destroy the bad spirits and replace them with the good spirits. The *Cinchona* tree-bark, for example, cures the "bad spirit" of malaria.

More than 120 prescription drugs are related to the medicinal plants of the Amazon. Of course, there are many "medicinal" herbs sold in popular markets—with unproven medicinal qualities. This is not the case with *Una de Gato*—Cat's Claw.

The Una de Gato—*Uncaria-tonticntosa*—is a tropical vine that grows in the rainforest and jungle of South America, including Peru. The vine gets its name from its curved thorns, found at the base of its oviform leaves, which resemble a cat's claw. These claws enable the vine to hold onto the host tree, climbing to heights of up to 40 meters (120 feet). Of the 13 known species of Una de Gato, only 3 contain medicinal properties—one of them is *Uncaria Mendosa.*

The *Ashanikas* tribe of Peru have the longest recorded history of using this plant. They have used it to treat the respiratory system, various forms of joint pain, recovery from childbirth, as a kidney cleanser, to cure deep wounds, alleviate stomach irritation, and to maintain a healthy cardiovascular system. Concentrated doses must be administrated by a qualified person to avoid health complications. I personally an unpleasant experience as a result of self-administrated concentrated doses of Una de Gato.

The Amazon Exploration Series *Constantine Issighos*

The Great Wonders of the Amazon

The Amazon Exploration Series　　　　　　　　　　　　　*Constantine Issighos*

The Great Wonders of the Amazon

The Amazon Exploration Series   *Constantine Issighos*

MEDICINAL PLANTS

The Amazon Exploration Series *Constantine Issighos*

The Great Wonders of the Amazon

www.ingramcontent.com/pod-product-compliance
Lightning Source LLC
Chambersburg PA
CBHW041755040426
42446CB00001B/38